Loving-kindness
Meditation

Loving-kindness Meditation

*Meditations to Help You Love Yourself, Love Others,
and Create More Love and Peace in the World*

by BILL SCHEFFEL *of the* NAROPA UNIVERSITY

FAIR WINDS
PRESS
GLOUCESTER, MASSACHUSETTS

Text © 2003 by Bill Scheffel

First published in the USA in 2003 by
Fair Winds Press
33 Commercial Street
Gloucester, MA 01930

Library of Congress Cataloging-in-Publication Data available

ISBN 1-59233-036-3

10 9 8 7 6 5 4 3 2 1

Printed and bound in China

Front cover image: Michael Kelley / Stone / Getty Images
Back cover image: L to R: Jennifer K. Beal, Wilkosz & Way, Carey Shaw
Designer: Mary Ann Guillette
Layout and Production: Jennifer K. Beal

Editorial Director: Donna Raskin
Managing Editor: Brigid Carroll
Photography Editor: Jennifer K. Beal

Excerpted text and poems include:

Arnold, Bob. "Is It" from *Once in Vermont*. © 1999 by Gnomon Press, Frankfort, Kentucky. Reprinted with permission.

Cohen, Leonard. "What Is A Saint?" from *Beautiful Losers* © 1993 by Vintage Books.

Gunaratana, Bhante Henepola, 2002. *Mindfulness in Plain English*. Wisdom Publications, Boston, MA.

Harjo, Joy. "I Give You Back" from *She Had Some Horses*. © 1983 by Thunder's Mouth Press, New York. Reprinted with permission.

Hulob, Miroslav. "Wings", translated by George Theiner, from *The Poetry of Survival: Post War Poets of Central and Eastern Europe*, edited by Daniel Weissbort. © 1991 by St. Martins Press, New York. Reprinted with permission.

From *Only Companion: Japanese Poems of Love and Longing*, translated by Sam Hamill, © 1997 by Sam Hamill. Reprinted by arrangement with Shambhala Publications, Inc., Boston, www.shambhala.com

Rinpoche, Sakyong Mipham, 2003. *Turning the Mind into an Ally*. Riverhead Books, New York.

Being Peace. ©1987 by Parale Press, Berkeley, CA.

Great Easter Sun: The Wisdom of Shambhala. ©1999 by Shambhala Publications, Inc, Boston, www.shambhala.com

Speaking of Silence: Christians and Buddhists on the Contemplative Way. Edited by Susan Walker. ©1987 by Paulist Press, New York.

This book is dedicated to my teacher,
Chögyam Trungpa Rinpoche
and to my mother and father.

❋ Table of Contents

INTRODUCTION

This book is a guide to the practice of loving-kindness. As a student of Buddhism and a practicing poet, each day I find loving-kindness to be at the center of both of these paths. As a teacher of meditation and creative writing, I try to begin classes by generating loving-kindness within myself and by extension, in the classroom. At home, with my partner, my son or my dog, there is not a single moment—whether or not I recognize the opportunity—when loving-kindness is unnecessary.

What is loving-kindness? Although a central teaching of Buddhism, loving-kindness is universal. The foundation of loving-kindness is acceptance of ourselves and others. My own teacher, Chögyam Trungpa Rinpoche, was once asked how to bring spiritual teachings to the man in the street. Trungpa's answer was to: *Start by just accepting the character of the person.* Even a violent temper or great laziness is not so much seen as an obstacle, but as a seed: *Since Buddha-nature pervades all beings, there is no such thing as an unsuitable candidate.*

In the West loving-kindness is associated with *agape*, which to the Greeks was the highest from of love, the selfless love, such as that of a mother for her child. Dr. Martin Luther King, Jr. called agape "a love that seeks nothing in return." "Agape," Dr. King wrote, "is an overflowing. When you rise to this level of love, you begin to love men, not because they are likable, but because God loves them." The New Testament is considered by many to contain the greatest teachings of loving-kindness.

The hard work of recognizing this Buddha-nature or love of God requires a step-by-step, day-by-day application of loving-kindness. This radical self-acceptance begins with ourselves. It occurs in the moment of rage when a dish breaks or when we fight with our wife, husband, or partner. It occurs in the dull depression of 1:00 P.M. after we've eaten too much for lunch but still have four hours before work is over. Loving-kindness is elusive. Often I feel I have none or know nothing about it. Like a shroud, self-criticism or resentment falls over us and self-kindness seems to vanish, but habitual patterns are by nature persistent and enveloping. If loving-kindness were easy, it would not be a practice. Training in loving-kindness helps us remember it when we most need it. And sometimes, just to remember it is enough to create a turning point within us.

Loving-kindness is our most noble social aspiration.

It is becoming clearer that there is less and less room for violent responses to fear and aggression. The sphere of our blue planet has only so much room for more suicide bombs, unexploded land mines, or depleted uranium bullets. Disrespect for our environment is a sign of diminished loving-kindness.

Merely striving for security through bigger weapons or more prisons is not the way of loving-kindness. Loving-kindness teaches that the core of the human heart is tender, and that behind the facades of racism, hatred, or religious fanaticism, are tears and a broken heart.

Buddhism
　　teaches
　that all beings possess
　　　　Buddha nature.

This Buddha nature
　　　—our human nature—
　is open,
　　awake and loving.

It is *basic goodness.*

CHAPTER 1 : Basic Goodness

To say that all people have a basic goodness conjures the question, "Are you sure?" Newspapers and other media show us a constant stream of anxiety, horrors and atrocities. The twentieth century was marked by a continuous series of small or large wars. Naturally, we are inclined to regard human beings as basically aggressive rather than good. But stories of war are seldom told outside the context of political propaganda or in full detail. Most men who have seen combat are horrified. Decades later, few soldiers are proud of the killing they have done. In his book, *War is a Force That Gives Us Meaning*, journalist Chris Hedges tells of a Muslim soldier who was fighting to take back a section of Sarajevo from Serbian control. In heavy combat he fired at an open doorway and killed a twelve-year-old girl. Hedges recounts that the man "saw the image of his own daughter. He broke down. He was lost for the rest of the war, shuttered inside his apartment, nervous, morose and broken." As horrible as this story is, it shows the man's heart was still tender and vulnerable.

Buddhist teachings admit that the habitual patterns of passion, aggression, and ignorance are strong. It is easy to become violent, even destroy our own life or the lives of others. But these patterns are momentary, motivated by fear. We find that what follows violence is regret; not necessarily guilt, but a sadness that we have strayed from the nature of our heart. Basic goodness teaches that our fundamental nature is beyond good and bad, it is an unconditioned state of being that, when contacted, expresses itself through an openness and a tenderness that is genuine and sad. Not a depressed sadness, but a sadness that feels our own and other's pain. If we uncover the truth of our heart, we find we want others to be happy and, like a mother's concern for her child, feel a motivation to help. Bringing attention to this "genuine heart of sadness" is one way to begin to develop loving-kindness.

May all beings enjoy happiness and the root of happiness.

Basic goodness occurs to us in simple moments of appreciation, moments in which we feel a connection of love with others. Pablo Neruda described one such moment when as a child he was playing in his backyard, "investigating the tiny objects and minuscule beings of my world." Absorbed in play, he came up against the boards of a fence; suddenly another small hand placed a tiny toy sheep in front of him, then disappeared.

Neruda never saw the child who gave him this wonderful gift, and he never forgot the incident, an act of selfless generosity. For Neruda, the incident "brought home to me for the first time the idea that all of humanity is somehow together. Maybe this small and mysterious exchange of gifts remained inside of me, deep and indestructible, giving my poetry light."

Wings

There is
the
microscopic
anatomy

of
the whale
this is
reassuring.

-WILLIAM CARLOS WILLIAMS

We have
a map of the universe
for microbes,
we have
a map of a microbe
for the universe.

We have
a Grand Master of chess
made of electronic circuits.

But above all
we have
the ability
to sort peas,
to cup water in our hands,
to seek
the right screw
under the sofa for hours.

This gives us
wings.

——MIROSLAV HOLUB
TRANS. GEORGE THEINER

Once my bitterness
has found its way into words,
it dissipates,
running deep into my heart
anger replaced by sadness.

—KYOGOKU TAMEKANE

CHAPTER 2: Meditation

Meditation is not necessarily a religious or spiritual activity. Like basic goodness, it is an innate and completely natural part of ourselves, but one we have lost touch with. Gary Snyder has written that meditation is "as fundamental a human activity as taking naps is to wolves or soaring in circles is to hawks and eagles." He calls meditation "attention to consciousness itself."

Buddhist traditions describe two aspects of meditation. The first is mindfulness, the process of settling and resting the mind. Mindfulness means being present rather than distracted by thoughts. Developing mindfulness leads to the second aspect, insight. With insight, also called awareness, we gradually come to recognize our Buddha nature or basic goodness. Mindfulness, literally resting the mind, is so fundamental to beginning to see what our nature is, that all spiritual disciplines—from the Lakota vision quest to the solitude of the fourth century Carmelite desert fathers—have probably contained methods to foster it. In the fundamental practice of being silent and still, it makes little difference whether we speak of the discoveries that occur as being mind, Buddha nature, God, spirit, or consciousness.

calm abiding

Normally, our mind is busy with thoughts and we are busy thinking about them, holding onto them, generating more of them. In this state we are distracted from life and distracted from ourselves. Mindfulness means calm abiding. Calm abiding is a way of letting thoughts subside. It is not an attempt to stop thought, just relax our involvement in the constant stream of thinking most of us do. The most common practice of mindfulness or calm abiding is sitting meditation. One sits in a comfortable position and begins by paying attention to the breath.

Sakyong Mipham Rinpoche, the son and lineage heir of Chögyam Trungpa Rinpoche, uses the term "peaceful abiding" for mindfulness, and describes the process succinctly:

In peaceful abiding we ground our mind in the present moment. We place our mind on the breath and practice keeping it there. We notice when thoughts and emotions distract us, and train in continually returning our mind to the breath. This is how we shift our alle-giance from the bewildered mind that causes its own suffering to the mind that is stable, clear and strong.

mindfulness

Mindfulness might seem very basic, even remedial. But once we begin, we find it to be challenging, exhilarating, and humbling. In meditation, we begin to really notice how many thoughts we have. This initial experience is described as sitting behind a waterfall. At times, the roar of discursive thoughts seems deafening. And the degree to which we are normally not mindful in daily life becomes more apparent to us. These experiences challenge us to call on the courage to persevere.

It is relatively easy to be mindful making love or hang gliding, but these activities occur between hours and hours of the mundane. Who really pays attention walking to the mail box or putting pots away? Yet our sense of wonder and loving-kindness is often born from the mundane. Who has not, at one time, watched dust particles float and dance in afternoon sunlight, and felt the vastness of the universe? Seemingly, we function so well, buying all the items on our shopping list and then placing them on the proper shelves of the refrigerator. But we are really only sleep-walking. We don't feel the sensuous cold of the perspiring milk carton, nor do we notice the lush ochre of stone-ground mustard. If we do not notice the things around us (much less other people), we cannot love them.

If we are fortunate enough to spend time with a master of meditation, we begin to see the penetrating and profound beauty of ordinary actions. And we see our own lack of mindfulness by contrast. For example, after almost twenty-five years of serious meditation, meditation teacher Sharon Salzberg began to study with Burmese Theravadan teacher U Pandita. As if she were a rank beginner, Pandita instructed Salzberg to takes notes describing the things she noticed after meditation. Salzberg's pride was soon undercut: "I'd go in there (for an interview) and before I could read my notes he'd say, 'What did you experience when you washed your face?' which was nothing, because I hadn't paid the least bit of attention to that."

By stilling our mind, the practice of mindfulness not only prepares us for the contemplation practices of loving-kindness, it also develops a great strength. When we attach to thoughts we find our mind is erratic and disturbed, blown this way and that. Mindfulness helps us to be steady and connected to where we are and who we are.

what is a saint?

A saint is someone who has achieved a remote human possibility. It is impossible to say what that possibility is. I think it has something to do with the energy of love. Contact with this energy results in the exercise of a kind of balance in the chaos of existence. A saint does not dissolve the chaos; if he did the world would have changed long ago. I do not think that a saint dissolves the chaos even for himself, for there is some-thing arrogant and warlike in the notion of a man setting the universe in order. It is a kind of balance that is his glory. He rides the drifts like an escaped ski. His course is the caress of the hill. His track is a drawing of the snow in a moment of its particular arrangement with wind and rock. Something in him so loves the world that he gives himself to the laws of gravity and chance. Far from flying with the angels, he traces with the fidelity of a seismograph needle the state of the solid, bloody landscape. His house is dangerous and finite, but he is at home in the world. He can love the shapes of human beings, the fine and twisted shapes of the heart. It is good to have among us such men, such balancing monsters of love.

—LEONARD COHEN

CHAPTER 3: Fear and Fearlessness

The mind of fearlessness should be put in the cradle of loving-kindness
—from the Shambhala text, *The Letter of the Black Ashe*

For most of us, the experience of fear is frequently stronger than the experience of basic goodness. This fear is not something that arises in the moment—such as when a car nearly hits us—but the internalized, psychological fear we each carry. This fear takes many shapes. Simple anxiety distracts us from ourselves, causing us to smoke, or eat too much chocolate. Severe emotional disorders or post-traumatic stress can produce crippling fear and equally strong methods of denial. Though admittedly difficult, the tradition of meditation teaches us that not only can fear be encountered, it must be encountered. James Baldwin wrote: "To defend oneself against a fear is simply to ensure that one will, one day, be conquered by it; fears must be faced." Encountering fear is the door that allows us to reach fearlessness. And the key to this door is the tool of loving-kindness.

The phrase, "The mind of fearlessness should be put in the cradle of loving-kindness," is an instruction for encountering our fear. This gesture of motherly love, of pure kindness, precedes all other actions. This metaphor provides a perfect model of how to treat ourselves in our most difficult experiences, such as when we experience fear. As the verb "put" implies, "the cradle of loving-kindness" is bigger than the fear. Fear can be included within this cradle, a psychological possibility bigger than our fear. This possibility is an attitude that we welcome our fear, that we host our fear. That, like a mother comforting a tearful child, we hold our fear. To develop the intention to welcome, to host or to hold our fear, is a very strong action. It is the first stop in discovering our basic goodness. The Vietnamese Buddhist teacher Thich Nhat Hanh has articulated many similar ways of confronting our fear. In one instruction he suggests talking to your fear, inviting it to join you: "Hello, my old friend fear, you have been with me for a long time. Now I see you again, please join me here."

I take myself back, fear.
You are not my shadow any longer.
I won't hold you in my hands.
You can't live in my eyes, my ears, my
voice
my belly, or in my heart my heart
my heart my heart

But come here, fear
I am alive and you are so afraid
　　　　of dying.

—FROM *I Give You Back*, BY JOY HARJO

feel your fear

Once we welcome or invite our fear, what then? The practice of mindfulness is the next tool. We attempt, instead of thinking about our fear, to feel the sensation—the felt sense—in our body. With mindfulness, one has a general awareness of what one's body is doing: sitting in meditation, opening the door, driving the car, eating, or walking. We can also become mindful of specific sensations. The taste of a tart apple is a tangible sensation, as is a hot washrag against our cheek. The breath is a more subtle sensation that we use as the basis of meditation practice. Fear and strong emotions always have an accompanying bodily sensation: a constriction in our chest, a rush of adrenaline, a queasiness in our stomach. When these sensations are strong, they are actually perfect candidates for mindfulness. They make becoming aware of them easy.

A good example of this is anger; something, like fear, that we find difficult. It is traditionally stated that anger—because it is so strong—is very easy to recognize with mindfulness. While this is true, the story line that accompanies anger normally pulls us into a turbulent stream of self-justifying discursive thought. But if we begin to practice the "felt sense," we develop the strength to turn our attention from our mental dialogue to the sensation in the body. Anger is inflated into rigid self-justification by our story line. Similarly, fears loom larger as we speculate about them. We must contact the felt sense of this fear or anger to simplify it. To realize that we can just feel fear or anger is a profound moment of loving-kindness. We discover that fear or anger is not necessarily against us, it just is. And since sensations always change, the felt sense of fear or anger does also. All emotions, since they are intense energies, eventually dissipate.

Experiencing our emotions through the direct sensation of their energy or felt sense leads to the fruition of mindfulness, what in Shambhala is called "synchronization of body and mind." Synchronization means to recognize that our perceptions occur prior to our concepts and ideas about them, our internal dialogue. As children, for example, we experienced the color red before learning the name "red." Likewise, when any of us see a blooming peony, we see pink before we name it, before we comment on it, or even like or dislike it. This perception before interpretation is almost instantaneous, but through meditation practice we begin to notice it. We begin to connect to things before language. As Trungpa Rinpoche said, "Intense emotions don't have a language. They are too intense in the first flash. After that, you begin to think, 'I hate you' or 'I love you.' Experiencing our emotions on this level is an immediate and profound experience of loving-kindness because it occurs before rejecting, or even accepting, them."

There is perhaps nothing more affirming than the self-acceptance that comes from realizing we can confront our own fears. As we practice "putting the mind of fearfulness in the cradle of loving-kindness" we progress on our path of developing fearlessness.

give yourself a break

That doesn't mean to say that you should drive to the closest bar and have lots to drink or go to a movie. Just enjoy the day, your normal existence. Allow yourself to sit in your home or take a drive into the mountains. Park your car somewhere; just sit; just be. It sounds very simplistic, but it has a lot of magic. You begin to pick up on clouds, sunshine and weather, the mountains, your past, your chatter with your grandmother and your grandfather, your mother, your father. You begin to pick up on a lot of things. Just let them pass like the chatter of a brook as it hits the rocks. We have to give ourselves some time to be.

We've been clouded by going to school, looking for a job—our lives are cluttered by all sorts of things. Your friends want you to come have a drink with them, which you don't want to do. Life is crowded with all sorts of garbage. In themselves, those things aren't garbage, but they're cumbersome when they get in the way of how to relax, how to be, how to trust, how to be a warrior. We've missed so many possibilities for that, but there are so many more possibilities that we can catch. We have to learn to be kinder to ourselves, much more kind. Smile a lot, although nobody is watching you smile. Listen to your own brook, echoing yourself. You can do a good job.

—CHÖGYAM TRUNGPA RINPOCHE

The Practice of Loving-kindness

The moon is a house
in which the mind is master.
Look very closely:
only impermanence lasts.
This floating world, too, will pass.

—IKKYU SOJUN

mantras

mantras

Although it is a foundation for discovering basic goodness, meditation is not the only way to find peace of mind. In both meditation and daily life, we can see the benefit of certain courses of action and then put them into practice. Since loving-kindness and compassion are part of the essence of basic goodness, we naturally want to reveal and develop these qualities in ourselves. The Buddhist tradition has evolved "slogans" that assist this process. One famous slogan is "Regard all dharmas as dreams." Dharmas in this case mean events. The slogan asks us to see that all events—from childbirth to getting the car tuned up—are transitory. Once gone, we have only a memory of them, no different than the memory of a dream. To regard life as a dream does not mean life is meaningless, as some people consider dreams to be. On the contrary, because all events in life are momentary and fleeting, they are all the more precious. We should meet them with loving-kindness.

be grateful to everyone

Another slogan that can help us open our heart to this fleeting world of our life is "Be grateful to everyone." In applying this, one doesn't start with the most extreme example possible—being grateful to a tyrant or murderer, for instance. Instead we focus on those we are in day-to-day contact with: parents, children, co-workers, the woman at the cash register. These are the people to whom we are often indifferent, frequently irritated with, and sometimes desire.

These attitudes—traditionally referred to as passion, aggression and ignorance—are all different than gratitude. The slogan not only reminds us to establish an open attitude toward others. Since we are often not open to the people in our life, "Be grateful to everyone" is a potent message. It reminds us that without these people we cannot develop loving-kindness!

you have to
appreciate yourself

It's quite organic. Plants, trees, and vegetables treat us that way. First they grow, and then they yield their fruit or themselves to be eaten. We cook them and make a good meal out of them. But human beings are usually more fishy; we haven't been able to yield to the fullest extent. We could actually become more like plants. First, just be—be a person—and then be a person to others. That kind of wanting to share, wanting to work with others is always there.

-TRUNGPA RINPOCHE

In these first stages, we typically begin with ourselves, which is entirely acceptable and recommended. We imagine a moment of happiness whose root is the experience of love or appreciation. Perhaps we think of the love we received from our mother or the smile of our young daughter when she first sees us in the morning. We might think of the pine tree outside our window, its beauty and strength.

CHAPTER 4: Loving-kindness Meditation

Like meditation, loving-kindness is a specific practice with a long history. Although the practice we will learn comes from the Buddhist tradition, it pre-dates the life of the Buddha; with ancient roots in Hinduism, loving-kindness practice is one of the four Bramaviharas or "limitless virtues." Loving-kindness is an aspiration for ourselves and all beings, and is translated, *May all beings enjoy happiness and the root of happiness*. Loving-kindness practice might be seen as the beginnings of a fire; the kindling, newspaper, and matches that can eventually grow into the kind of selfless love the saints and bodhisattvas have. Without loving-kindness, it is difficult to become grateful to a boss we don't really like. So we start—as Trungpa Rinpoche constantly advised—at the beginning.

Loving-kindness is a contemplation practice. Unlike sitting meditation, in which we let go of thought and return to the breath or sensation in the body, contemplation is attention on a thought. It is necessary to have some training in meditation before beginning contemplation practice. Meditation gives us the strength to be mindful and mindfulness leads to the experience of peace. With mindfulness, we can contemplate a specific thought, rather than becoming discursive, our usual experience. When our thinking becomes discursive, our thoughts come and go like so many stray radio stations. Placing our attention on a specific thought is little different than placing it on the breath.

step one:

Begin with at least five minutes of sitting meditation.
Having engaged in the practice of mindfulness, we begin
to settle our mind and provide a foundation to build on.

step two:

Invoke the aspiration of loving-kindness by saying to
yourself, "May all beings enjoy happiness and the root of
happiness." In order to contact the "root" of happiness,
imagine a situation of happiness.

step three:

The practice of loving-kindness is like a series of concentric circles radiating out. We begin with what is both easy and close at hand; ourselves and our own experience. Now we think of someone who is alive today and with whom we have a good relationship. It is easy to want to wish this person happiness. Imagine the feelings of happiness and loving-kindness that we've already generated as a kind of tangible energy we radiate to this person. Imagine her experiencing a similar happiness. Once again, use your imagination to embellish the person; make her real in your mind and radiate loving-kindness to her.

step four:

Now try radiating loving-kindness to someone you feel neutral about; perhaps the mailman or neighbor three doors down. You might also choose to include those with whom you are uncomfortable, even an enemy. Let the practice be natural, do not force yourself to go where you don't wish to. The point in step four is simply to expand the circle again, to begin to include people who are not usually of concern to us. Sometimes I try to simply remember those people who were in my life the previous day; someone in my poetry class or the woman at the supermarket checkout. Often I find just remembering someone makes them suddenly precious.

step five:

Now we may expand the circle as far as we like. In this stage the radiation of loving-kindness becomes less specific. We imagine both our conscious intention and the tangible energy of loving-kindness radiating in all directions. It goes out to the trees and birds in our yard, across the state line into Nebraska, Arizona, Virginia; across the world to Tokyo or Mexico City. We begin to see all beings included in loving-kindness. If we are convinced others want happiness in ways similar to us, whom can we exclude? You may radiate the circle as far as your imagination and inclination may go: your neighborhood, the earth, the solar system, the galaxy. Even "limitless space." To end, you might repeat the slogan,

"May all beings enjoy happiness and the root of happiness."

These five steps are not meant to make the practice complex and are certainly not meant to make it rigid. Remember, this is a natural practice, your practice. Only you can make it real. The essence of the practice is to: let the mind settle; imagine people, animals or events that give rise to kindness and love; feel and then become the essence of what moves you; and radiate the essence of this as loving energy to other people and beings.

Sometimes we find we cannot generate real feelings. We feel robotic or numb. At other times we might experience the opposite of loving-kindness: fear, hesitation, jealousy, or rage. Remember that these experiences are natural and part of the journey. Like the encounter with fear, whatever arises can be met and explored. It is enough to simply remain interested. To be curious is a gesture of loving-kindness. To accept the negative is a gesture of loving-kindness. Do what you can. Use your own judgment. Do not force yourself.

CHAPTER 5: RE-active

So far, we've described loving-kindness contemplation as a formal practice. This daily, formal activity—a priority we begin the day with—is very powerful, all the more so when done consistently. A session of meditation and contemplation establishes this intention in our mind. As we remember this intention, we find unexpected, and less formal, opportunities to practice loving-kindness during our daily life. And there are more opportunities than we realize. While riding the bus or waiting for the dentist, we can contemplate loving-kindness.

When an image we are contemplating begins to move us, we may feel a sensation in our body; perhaps a warmth in the area of our heart or slight release of constriction in our chest. We allow ourselves to feel the happiness in our mind and, if possible, in our body. It is possible to become it, to be it. The feeling might last for only a moment, but that is adequate; even a split second of real happiness—with its potential for love—is enough to begin to open us, to turn our mind in the direction of loving-kindness. Think to yourself, "May I experience the well-being of happiness now and in the future."

My fiftieth year had come and gone,
I sat, a solitary man,
In a crowded London shop,
An open book and empty cup
On the marble table-top

While on the shop and street I gazed
My body of a sudden blazed;
And twenty minutes more or less
It seemed, so great my happiness,
That I was blessed and could bless.

—WILLIAM BUTLER YEATS

-excerpt from <u>Vacillation</u>

Your meditation should revive & relax you. If it becomes stale, make it vivid.

Contemplation is not effective if it remains dry or remedial, like reciting a list of rules. Contemplation combines the imagination and mindfulness into a potent force. It is personal. We contact images from our own heart and bring them to life with mindfulness. The point is to *see it, feel it,* and *become it.* An image I sometimes use is from a trip my son and I took to Death Valley, California, when he was six. Driving at night, we came upon a huge sand dune at the side of the deserted highway.

The moon was full, and I suddenly had the inspiration to take off all our clothes and run through the sand. I suggested this to my son, who gleefully agreed. After thirty minutes of running, jumping, and rolling down the sand dunes he said to me, "This is the best time I've ever had."

This memory easily brings tears to my eyes. It connects my own happiness with my son's happiness.

May all beings enjoy happiness and the root of happiness.

May they be free from suffering and the the root of suffering.

May they not be seperated from the great happiness devoid of suffering.

May they dwell in the great equamity free from passion, aggression,

and ignorance.

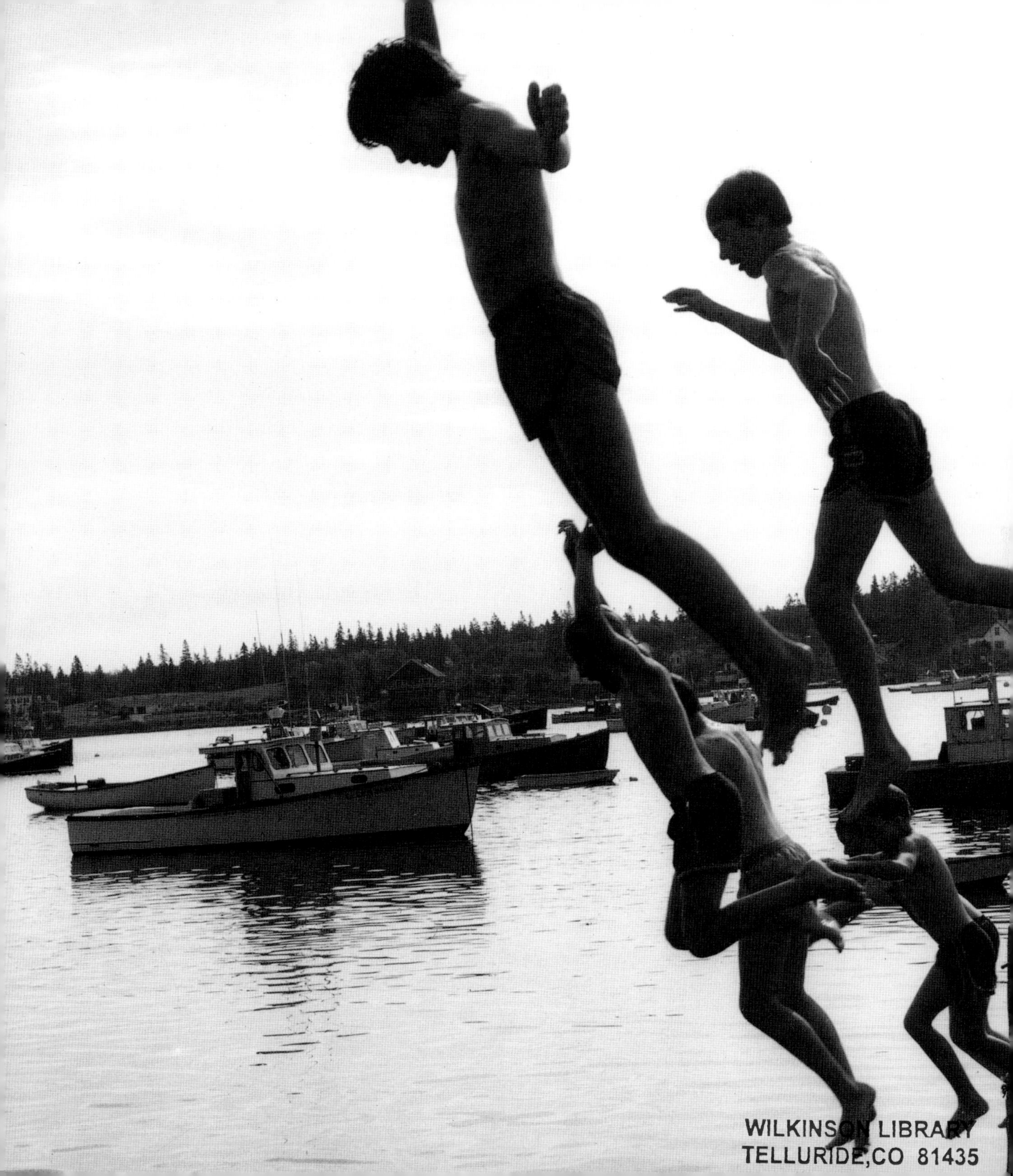

My Beloved is the Mountains
And lonely wooded valleys,
Strange islands,
And resounding rivers,
The whistling of love-stirring
breezes,

The tranquil night
At the time of the rising dawn,
Silent music,
Sounding solitude,
The supper that refreshes, and
deepens love.

—SAINT JOHN OF THE CROSS

CHAPTER 6: "Changing" Ourselves

Meditation gives us the experience of simply being with ourselves. We allow thoughts and feelings to occur. We do not judge them and we do not hold onto them. Meditation is a practice of minimum interference and maximum allowance of experience. Similarly, the practice of loving-kindness is one of developing sympathy for ourselves and, by extension, others. Of course, we do find ourselves judging and forcing our experience, but we gradually gain recognition that this does not help and is not the point. We begin to let go.

Part of letting go is in fact letting go of the desire to change ourselves. If we think only of change, we miss the glimpse of basic goodness, our fundamental nature, which does not need to be changed. Instead of changing ourselves, we try to become curious and sympathetic to our experience. If we are merely trying to change, we are caught in spiritual desire. We are involved in gamesmanship with ourselves, trying to abandon a "bad self" and latch onto a "good one."

{ You are. Fine. }

Using Spiritual Practice to force self-change is a subtle form of self-aggression. Pema Chödren describes the inner dialogue this aggression might take: "If I could meditate and calm down, I'd be a better person," or "If it weren't for my husband, I'd have a perfect marriage." Even these internal conversations are not "bad." In fact, recognizing them brings a sense of humor, itself a form of acceptance and loving-kindness.

Whenever we are able to laugh at ourselves, loving-kindness is near at hand. Rather than the fulfillment of a longed-for future change, loving-kindness contemplation is based on revealing and developing our innate qualities now.

The Buddha said, "By surveying the entire world with my mind, I have not come across anyone who loves others more than himself. Therefore, one who loves himself should cultivate this loving-friendliness." Cultivate loving-friendliness toward yourself first, with the intention of sharing your kind thoughts with others. Develop this feeling; be full of kindness toward yourself. Accept yourself just as you are. Make peace with your shortcomings. Embrace even your weaknesses. Be gentle and forgiving with yourself as you are at this very moment. If thoughts arise as to how you should be such and such a way, let them go. Establish fully the depth of these feelings and goodwill and kindness. Let the power of loving-friendliness saturate your entire body and mind; relax in its warmth and radiance. Expand this feeling to your loved ones, to people you don't know or feel neutral about—and even to your adversaries!

—BHANTE HLENEPOLA GUNARATANA

If you have any doubt about whether you are doing the meditation practice right or wrong, it doesn't matter all that much. The main point is to have honesty within yourself. Just do what you think is best. That is called self-truth. If truth is understood by oneself, then you cannot be persecuted at all, karmically or any other way. You're doing your best, so what can go wrong?

Cheer up and have a good time.

—CHÖGYAM TRUNGPA RINPOCHE

four sublime states

Loving-friendliness is one of the four sublime states defined by the Buddha, along with compassion, appreciative joy, and equanimity. The ultimate goal of our practice of meditation is the cultivation of these four sublime states.

One way to understand them is to think of different stages of parenthood. When a young woman finds out she is going to have a child, she feels a tremendous outpouring of love for her baby. The feeling a new mother has for her infant is limitless and all-embracing, and does not depend on the actions or behavior of the one receiving her thoughts of loving-friendliness.

As the infant grows older and starts to explore his world, the parents develop compassion. Every time the child falls down, the parent feels the child's pain. Compassion leads us to appropriate action; the pure, heartfelt hope that the pain will stop and the child not suffer.

As time passes, the child heads off to school. Parents watch as the youngster makes friends, does well in school and sports. The parents are not jealous or resentful of their child's success but are full of happiness for the child. This is appreciative joy. Even when we think of others whose success exceeds our own, we can appreciate their achievement and rejoice in their happiness.

Eventually, after many years, the child grows up. He finishes school and goes out on his own; perhaps he marries and starts a family. Of course the parents continue caring for and respecting their child, but they do so with awareness that they no longer steer the outcome of their child's life. This is the practice of equanimity.

—ADAPTED FROM BHANTE HENEPOLA GUNARATANA

slowness

Part of developing sympathy for ourselves—not to mention simply enjoying our life—is to acknowledge the speed and craving that is part of the modern, industrialized world. Each year, the pace of the demands around us seems to increase, as does the toll it takes. Writer Noelle Oxenhandler cites riding passenger trains through the French countryside as one of the supreme pleasures of her life. Recently, she traveled again in France, but the old trains had been replaced by high speed ones that moved so fast she found it impossible to watch the countryside. Travel is no longer leisurely, but a rush from one place to the next.

We have all internalized the frenetic momentum around us. Speed makes it easy to become aggressive and difficult to feel loving-kindness. It is doubtful we can develop mindfulness and loving-kindness without slowing the pace of our lives. It's not that we can change the speed limit from sixty-five miles-per-hour back down to fifty, or extend the deadlines our boss imposes on us. What we can do is slow the inner momentum. If we begin to breathe deeply, for instance, while in rush-hour, bumper-to-bumper traffic, or waiting in line at the bank, we transform frustration into attention to our world—that is loving-kindness!

smile

Sometimes the spirit leads, and sometimes the body can lead. This is why, when you have joy, you naturally smile. But sometimes you can allow the smile to go first. You try to smile and suddenly you feel that you don't suffer that much any more. So don't discriminate against the body. The body also can be a leader, not only the spirit. I propose that you try this when you wake up during the night. It's totally dark. Breathe in and smile, and you'll see. Smile to life. You are alive, you smile. This is not a diplomatic smile, because no one sees you smiling. Yet the smile is a smile of enlightenment, of joy—the joy you feel of being alive.

Thich Nhat Hanh teaches a wonderful practice for slowing down and developing cheerful sympathy. It is called the "half-smile" practice. I've practiced it and taught it to students for years, and it works! It is a mindfulness-in-daily-life practice that involves simply remembering to smile. The smile we adopt is subtle; perhaps barely noticeable to someone else (hence the term half-smile). Somehow, the physical effect of smiling (done with mindfulness) can shift our inner mood. Thich Nhat Hahn explains why this is a practice: "Smiling is a practice, a yoga practice. Don't say, 'I have no joy, why do I have to smile?' Because when you have joy and you smile, that is not practice, that's very natural. When you don't have joy and you smile, that is a real practice."

Is It

river
flowing
beneath
the stars

or stars
flowing
over the
river

——BOB ARNOLD

So we have to learn to smile and then we'll look presentable right away. Look into the mirror and practice, and you'll see that the practice of the smile is very important. It brings relaxation and you can let go. You feel that you are released from the grip of the anger, or the despair. When you walk in the hills, or in a park, or along a river bank, you can follow your breath, with a half-smile blooming on your lips. When you feel tired or irritated, you can lie down with your arms at your sides, allowing all your muscles to relax, maintaining awareness of just your breath and your smile.

Relaxing in this way is wonderful, and quite refreshing. You will benefit a lot if you practice it several times a day. Your mindful breath and your smile will bring happiness to you and to those around you. Even if you spend a lot of money on gifts for everyone in your family, nothing you could buy them can give as much true happiness as your gift of awareness, breathing, and smiling, and these precious gifts cost nothing.

—Thich Nhat Hanh

Smiling helps us let go. Almost as if by magic, it can pull us from our thought-obsessing mind and into the present moment. Remembering to breathe or simply looking around us—at the trees, the sky, even the traffic—are similarly powerful. Fundamentally, we are training ourselves to be and not always do. Even the practice of loving-kindness could become an obsession. Quite simply, we must relax. Trungpa Rinpoche advised us, give yourself time to be. "You're not going to see the Shambhala vision, you're not even going to survive, by not leaving yourself a minute to be, a minute to smile."

photography credits

Photography by Helen J. Beal: 67

Photography by Jennifer K. Beal: 1, 5, 15, 25, 35, 39, 45, 51, 53, 61, 73, 89, 95, 96
www.jkbealphoto.com

Photography by Kenneth L. Beal: 69

Photography by Digital Vision/Getty Images: 21, 29, 31, 33, 41, 49, 57

Photography by Bas Hoeben: 4, 65

Photography courtesy of the Johnston Collection: 11

Photography by Keller & Keller: 43
www.kellerkeller.com

Photography by Photodisc/Getty Images: 9, 55, 63, 71, 77, 81, 85

Photography by Carey Shaw: 27, 75
www.careyshaw.com

Photography by Stockbyte/Picturequest: 13, 19, 23, 47, 83, 87, 93

Photography by Wilkosz & Way: 17, 37, 59, 79
www.wilkoszandway.com